Also by Doug Marlette

The Emperor Has No Clothes

If You Can't Say Something Nice

Drawing Blood

It's a Dirty Job but Somebody Has to Do It

Kudzu

Preacher

Just a Simple Country Preacher

Chocolate Is My Life

There's No Business Like Soul Business

Shred This Book

I Am Not a Televangelist!

Til Stress Do Us Part

A Doublewide with a View

In Your Face

EVEN *White* BOYS get the Blues

Kudzu's First Ten Years

by
Doug Marlette
Introduction by Pat Conroy

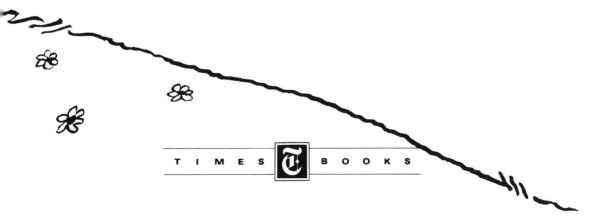

TIMES 𝕋 BOOKS

All rights reserved under International and Pan-American Copyright Conventions.
Published in the United States by Times Books, a division of Random House, Inc., New York,
and simultaneously in Canada by Random House of Canada Limited, Toronto.

All of the cartoons that appear in this work have been previously published in various newspapers.
"Kudzu" is distributed by Creators Syndicate, Inc.

Library of Congress Cataloging-in-Publication Data

Marlette, Doug
Even white boys get the blues: Kudzu's first ten years / Doug
Marlette; introd. by Pat Conroy. - 1st ed.
p. cn.
ISBN 0-8129-2072-4
I. Title.
PN6728. K8M3685 1992
741.5'973 — dc20   92-53665

Color design and hand coloring by Dizzy Fish Studios, Siesta Key, Florida.

Manufactured in the United States of America

9 8 7 6 5 4 3 2

First Edition

*For Mack Ray,
who recognized the spark
and provided kindling instead of
dousing it.
With gratitude.*

Introduction

By Pat Conroy

When I was a boy, a comic book was the only place I could turn to make any sense of the world. Cartoons were my tickets to the pleasures of language, and the comic books I collected as a child were my first introductions to the joys and complications of literature. Cartoonists have spoken to me in ways that Jackson Pollock never will. I take cartooning seriously. As an adult, when I wandered through a cavern near the Dordogne River in France, I marveled at the paintings of Cro-Magnon men who lived there thousands of years before Christ. I was deeply moved by the work of the Earth's first artists, by their reproductions of herds of bison, deer, horses and mammoths flowing eternally across acres of stone. A guide revealed a secret to me that Doug Marlette has known since birth. "They are cartoons," she said.

A cartoon is an approximation and an exaggeration or a dilution of the true image, but so is every other art form. A cartoon is to art what schizophrenia is to human composure. Though it is the meeting ground between literature and the fine arts, cartoons have always been the bastard child in the attic. They are Cinderella cleaning up in the kitchen when the family of fine artists has gone to bed. No one, except perhaps a child, feels completely comfortable with cartoons; a caricature, after all, is a human being rendered conceivable.

Of the cartoon strips being drawn in America today, *Kudzu* is my favorite. It is also the first to come out of the American South that celebrates the Southern experience. Al Capp once made fun of the rural South with Li'l Abner, but Marlette has created the first comic strip that is Southern in its nature, temperament, and design. When you read *Even White Boys Get the Blues,* you are solidly placed in the New South in all its fullness and ludicrousness and its stumbling and hilarious attempts to fit into the modern world. The cartoon's Southernness is both its glory and its built-in affliction.

Marlette writes and draws about the South as though it were not a major crime to be Southern. Sometimes newspaper editors in the North and the West use this as an excuse not to run the strip. It is as if *Kudzu,* by owning up to the particularity of its origins, makes itself unworthy of inclusion in other geographical quadrants. Even though Marlette's characters are as original and universal of those of Charles Dickens, he has harmed himself by remaining true to his Southern heritage. If he wrote about Bypass, America, instead of Bypass, North Carolina, he would be syndicated in every newspaper in the country. But *Kudzu* is Southern by nature and preference, and so is Marlette.

Doug Marlette, son of Aquarius, baby boomer, left-hander, Carolinian, Southerner, and lifelong enthusiast, has often acted as the carotid artery of his generation, carrying the blood supply to the brain for all of us. His political cartoons have set the standard for the last twenty years, and he won the Pulitzer Prize for Editorial Cartooning in 1988. His political cartoons often cause extreme discomfort, raise the blood pressure, and more than once have caused people to fling their newspapers across the room in outrage. Marlette has inspired every single range of passions and emotions except indifference. He lives solidly in the heart of the matter. His homeland, in the arts, is center court. When he draws a political cartoon, it seems to burst out of a great sea within him, like Moby Dick sounding near the *Pequod* from up out of the depths. They are deeply lived-in things, and they are composed of fire and blood and fury. Though much arouses his heightened sense of awe and pity, almost everything inspires his laughter. Where restraint should reside in Marlette's central nervous system, a pixilated sense of the absurd winks dangerously as radium. Like all good cartoonists, he would be shot by order of the dictator in a totalitarian state. Even in our own democracy, some politicians believe that shooting would be too good for Marlette.

There is much about the history of cartooning I don't know, but I know a novel in progress when I see one. And I know very well how autobiography can intrude and interject and insinuate itself into an artist's work. When all these cartoon strips are one day gathered into a grand and sprawling collection, one will be able to trace the lineaments and far corners and dark dimensions of Doug Marlette's life. This book has the feeling and the markings of the *bildungsroman,* the coming-of-age novel. It shares similarities with *Look Homeward, Angel* or *David Copperfield.*

Kudzu expresses what Doug Marlette sees happening in our country right now. This collectionof his comic strips is a splendid introduction to what Marlette believes about philosophy, religion, athletics, race relations, the sexual revolution, small-town life, politics – all laced with an overriding humor that makes Marlette one of the great comic forces of our time. There is nothing Marlette will not laugh at; he lines up sacred cows for the equally sacred pleasure of knocking them down. Everything is fair game, and anything that catches Marlette's interest in society eventually shows up in *Kudzu*.

The artist begins with nothing at all, then must make his mark on the world. The cartoonist faces an arctic landscape everyday of his life. By lines and words, Marlette defines himself and tells his story. Love is hard to find in Bypass, North Carolina, and the groping toward God is the longest and most notable of all of mankind's odysseys.

With this collection of *Kudzu*'s first ten years, I welcome you to Bypass and into the lives of Kudzu Dubose and Will B. Dunn and Uncle Dub and Veranda Tadsworth and all the others. Each character in *Kudzu* is both singularly imagined and archetypal at the same time. Doug Marlette has created a world of the first order by following his own first urging toward art.

3

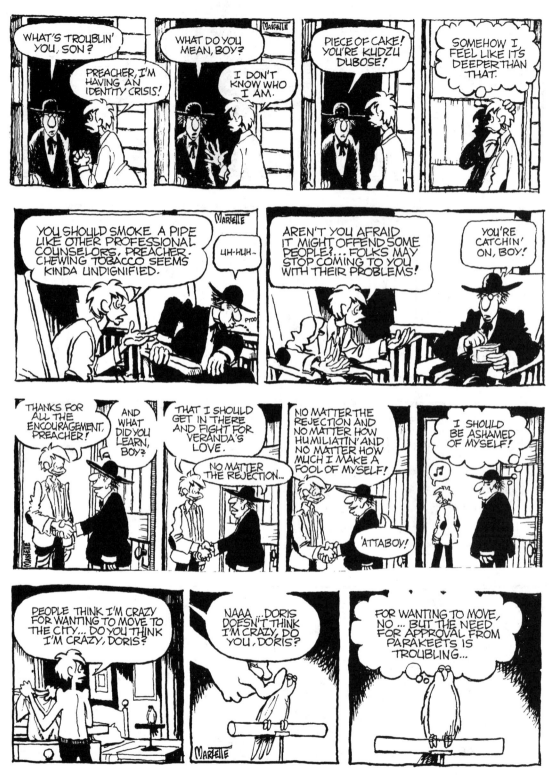

10

15

16

17

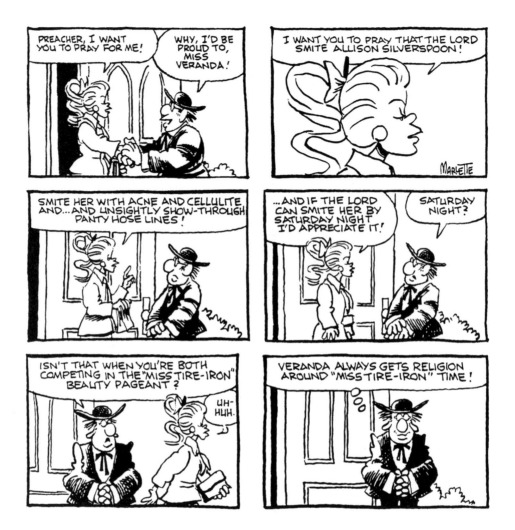

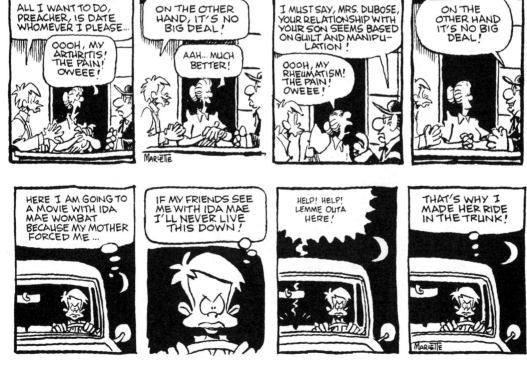

22

23

29

30

33

36

41

44

48

52

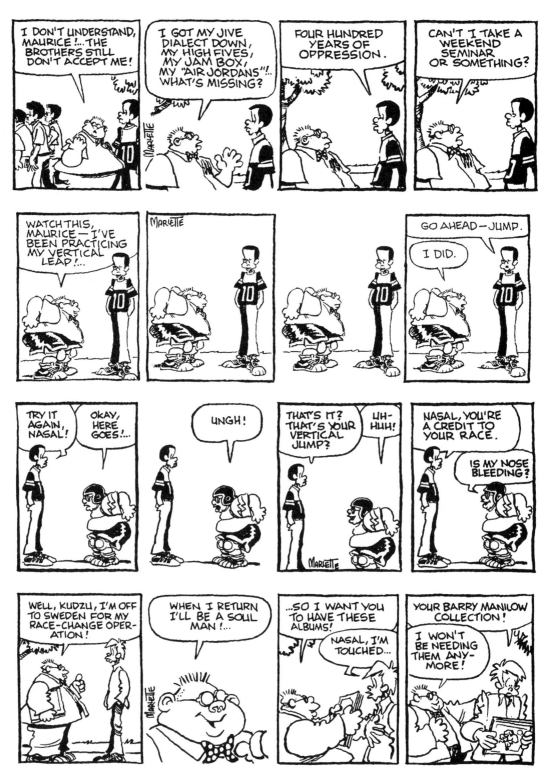

54

56

57

58

HERE SHE COMES!

VERANDA, WILL YOU GO OUT WITH ME.

NO.

IT'S BECAUSE I HAVE NO CHEST HAIR, ISN'T IT?

YOU HAVE NO CHEST HAIR?

⸮SIGH⸮ NO.

ACTUALLY, KUDZU, SOME WOMEN FIND MEN WITH SMOOTH, HAIRLESS CHESTS VERY SEXY...

REALLY.

OH, YES.

THEN WILL YOU GO OUT WITH ME.

NO.

OH NO! HERE COMES IDA MAE! SHE'S GONNA ASK ME OUT AGAIN!...

...AND I'M RUNNING OUT OF GOOD EXCUSES FOR TURNING HER DOWN!

BING BONG

HI, KUDZU! WHAT DO YOU SAY WE GO TO A MOVIE SATURDAY NIGHT?!

UH...UH... UMM...ER...

EXCUSE ME, IDA MAE! I GOTTA MAKE A QUICK PHONE CALL!

HELLO, VERANDA? WILL YOU GO OUT WITH ME SATURDAY NIGHT?

AW, GEE, KUDZU, I'D LOVE TO, BUT I'M REWINDING MY VIDEOS!

AW, GEE, IDA MAE, I'D LOVE TO, BUT I'M REWINDING MY VIDEOS!

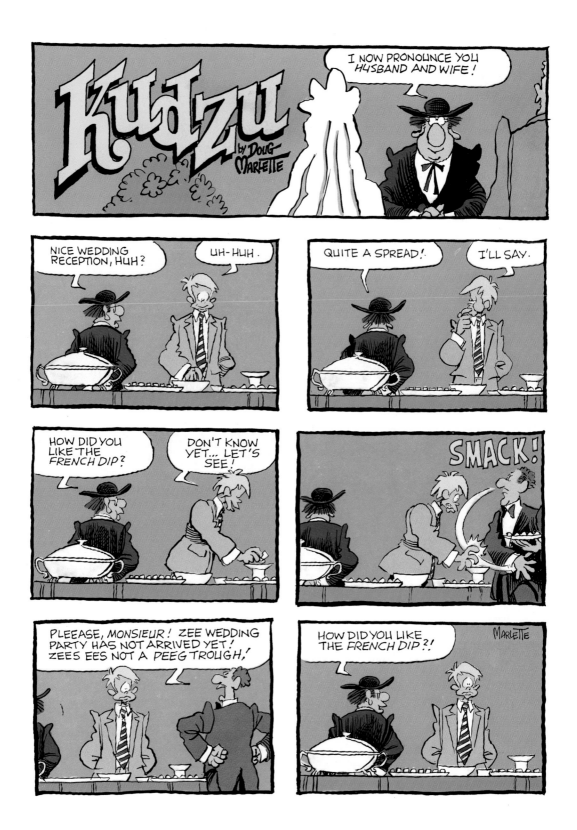

Kudzu by Doug Marlette

...AND NOW A GUY WHO NEEDS NO INTRODUCTION !...

MY GUEST TODAY ON THE EVE OF HIS FAMOUS SOJOURN IS THE LEGENDARY SANTA CLAUS !...

HO, HO, HO!

SANTA, LET'S TAKE THE GLOVES OFF, SHALL WE ?...

YOU KNOW WHEN WE'VE BEEN SLEEPING... YOU KNOW WHEN WE'RE AWAKE... YOU'RE MAKING A LIST... CHECKING IT TWICE... GONNA FIND OUT WHO'S NAUGHTY OR NICE... TELL ME, DOES THE CONSTITUTIONAL RIGHT TO PRIVACY MEAN ANYTHING TO YOU?!...

BUT FIRST, TELL US, IS RUDOLPH'S RED NOSE DUE TO HIS BEING IN *REHAB*?

...AND FROSTY THE SNOWMAN— HE'S A CRACK *DEALER*, RIGHT?!

...AND ONE MORE THING : HAVE YOU EVER SEXUALLY HARASSED AN ELF?!

HEY—WHAT DO YOU WANT?!... I'M ON HEAD TO HEAD WITH GERALDO?!

NASAL T. LARDBOTTOM IS AN ASPIRING *BROTHER*:

HE IS FLUENT IN *JIVE*:

YO MAMA! WHAT IT BE! I AIN'T PLAYIN' WITCHA!

HE CAN *HIGH-FIVE* WITHOUT INJURING HIMSELF... (OR OTHERS.)

HE HAS MASTERED INTRICATE GREETINGS AND HAND-SHAKES...

MY MAN!

HE HAS WORN *DASHIKIS* TO SCHOOL

WE BAD!

...AND HE EVEN UNDERWENT AN UNSUCCESSFUL RACE-CHANGE OPERATION AND SOUL IMPLANT PROCEDURE...

PHOOEY!

...BUT HOW IS HIS AMBITION AND DRIVE REWARDED?

NASAL T. LARDBOTTOM

WHITEST WHITE BOY

STAY TUNED...

NATURALLY, I'M PLEASED WE'VE HAD AN INCREASE IN THE NUMBER OF BAPTISMS LATELY...

...BUT I WANT TO ASK OUR YOUNG PEOPLE TO PLEASE REFRAIN FROM REFERRING TO OUR SACRED ORDINANCE OF BAPTISM AS:

"...POOL PARTIES."

*V*OTED "WHITEST WHITE BOY" AT BYPASS HIGH FOR AN UNPRE-CEDENTED SECOND STRAIGHT YEAR NASAL DOES WHAT ANY RED-BLOODED AMERI-CAN DOES WHEN TRAGEDY STRIKES: HE HITS THE TALK SHOWS!

TV

BACK-TO-BACK "WHITE BOYS"! NASAL, TELL US— HOW DID YOU DO IT?

I DON'T UNDERSTAND, PREACHER— I SPEAK JIVE FLUENTLY!...I MEMORIZED ALL THE MOTOWN LYRICS!...

I ZEROXED MY HAND, TAPED IT TO THE WALL, AND POUNDED MY FINGERS TO A BLOODY PULP PRACTICING MY *HIGH FIVES!*

THAT'S A WHITE BOY ALL RIGHT!

NASAL, YOU SEEM OBSESSED WITH YOUR SKIN COLOR AS A KEY TO YOUR HAPPINESS!

I MEAN, CAN'T YOU BE HIP, FUNKY, UNINHIBITED AND SECURE IN YOUR DUDENESS AND STILL REMAIN A WHITE BOY?

WE TALK SHOW HOSTS ARE NOTED FOR OUR SHALLOWNESS!

62

63

PREACHER'S HEALING OF NASAL'S LIMP COIFFURE DOESN'T LAST:

DROOOOP

...WHEN HE UTTERS THE INCANTATION: *PRESIDENT DAN QUAYLE!*

SPROING!

...HIS HAIR STANDS ON END!

...MOMENTARILY...

DROOOOP

...YET NOBODY CAN CONTEMPLATE SUCH A PROSPECT FOR VERY LONG!

PRESIDENT DAN QUAYLE!

SPROING

...WITHOUT THE RISK OF DAMAGE TO THE CENTRAL *NERVOUS* SYSTEM!

DROOOP

SO EVEN NASAL'S DESPERATE DREAM TO BE ACCEPTED BY THE BROTHERS MUST FACE THE AWFUL TRUTH:

I'M STUCK WITH THE *BORING* HAIR OF A *WHITE BOY* FOREVER!

NASAL'S GOT A RIGHT TO SING THE BLUES!

WELL, MY 'DO IT WAS RIGHTEOUS, IT WAS FINE AS CAN BE! 'TIL THAT FADE IT DONE FADED... IT WENT **AWOL** ON ME!

DOUBLECROSSED BY MY HAIRSTYLE, AN' MY PRIDE IT GOT MAULED... BACKSTABBED BY MY FOLLICLES... MIGHT AS WELL WAKE UP BALD!

I GOTS DEM DOUBLE CROSSIN, WHO'S DE BOSSIN', HALF-MAST'N', FADIN FAST'N' DON'T CARE, WHITE BOY HAIR BETRAYED-BY-YO'-FADE LOW DOWN, HIGH-TOP BLUES!

HOLY CATFISH! WHAT'S THAT *PUDDLE*?!

UH—THE RINGBEARER WAS SO NERVOUS HE TINKLED ON THE FLOOR!

OH, GOOD...

I WAS AFRAID IT WAS *MINE!*

KUDZU, LET'S TALK ENGAGEMENT RINGS!

THAT DOES IT!

I DON'T WANNA TALK ENGAGEMENT RINGS, IDA MAE! I DON'T WANNA TALK AT ALL! IN FACT, I'D BE THRILLED IF I NEVER HAD TO TALK TO YOU EVER AGAIN!

FINE—IF THAT'S THE WAY YOU FEEL ABOUT IT!

YOU'RE DARN TOOTIN' THAT'S THE WAY I FEEL ABOUT IT!

...THEN LET'S DISCUSS SILVER PATTERNS!

74

75

80

82

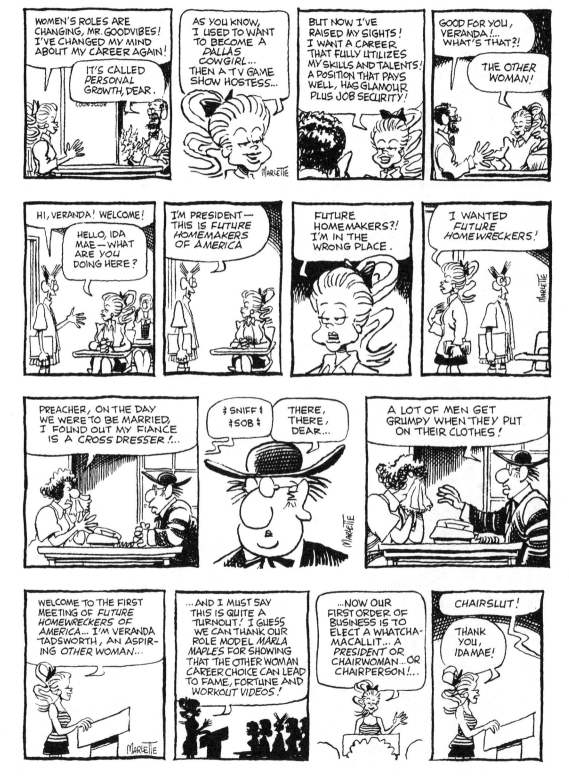

90

91

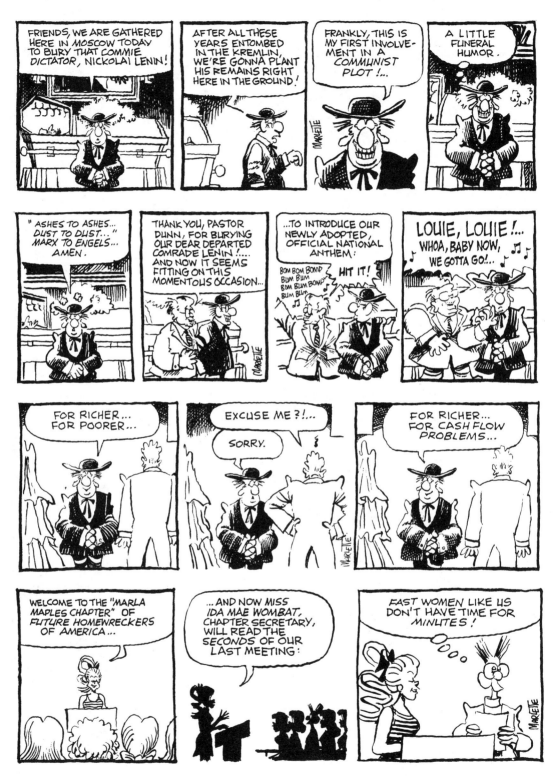

93

95

97

99

100

103

...and a skateboard and a soccer ball...

By the way, Santa, I don't care what anybody says...

I still believe in you.

Sincerely, Jad

P.S. And a Milli Vanilli album.

DUB, WHY DON'T YOU COME TO OUR CHRISTMAS PAGEANT THIS YEAR?

DREAM ON, PREACHER!

AW, C'MON, DUB! WHERE'S YOUR CHRISTMAS SPIRIT?

I DON'T DARKEN YOUR DOOR ALL YEAR LONG, PREACHER...

...IT'D BE MIGHTY HYPOCRITICAL OF ME TO SHOW UP ON HOLIDAYS ONLY...

IF THERE'S ONE THING Y'ALL DON'T NEED OVER THERE IT'S ANY MORE HYPOCRITES!

THAT'S RIGHT THOUGHTFUL OF YOU, DUB!

... AND NOW TO HELP GET YOU INTO THE HOLIDAY SPIRIT...

... SOME HOLIDAY IMPRESSIONS:

FROSTY, THE SNOWBIRD!

HOW GOES REHEARSAL FOR THE CHRISTMAS PAGEANT, PREACHER?

DON'T ASK.

VERANDA INSISTS ON PLAYING THE VIRGIN MARY AGAIN THIS YEAR!

IT DEFINITELY DISTRACTS FROM THE MOOD OF A MANGER SCENE WHEN THE VIRGIN MARY IS TWIRLING A FIRE BATON!

104

105

107

109

111

112

113

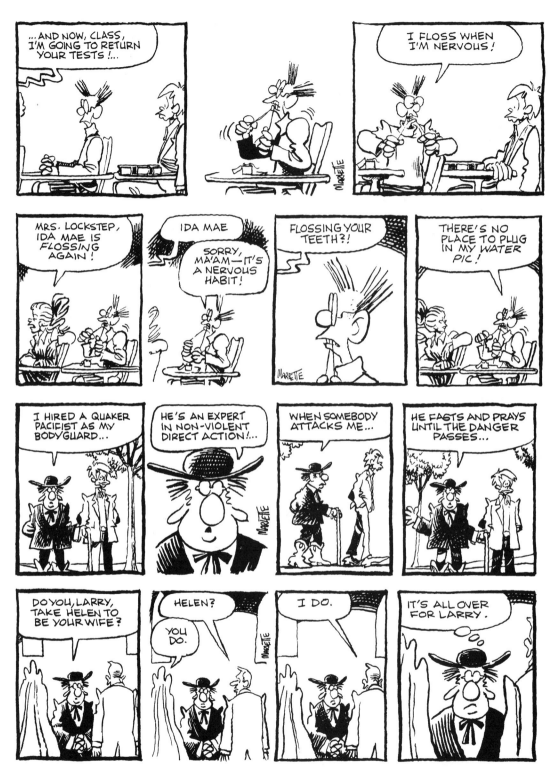

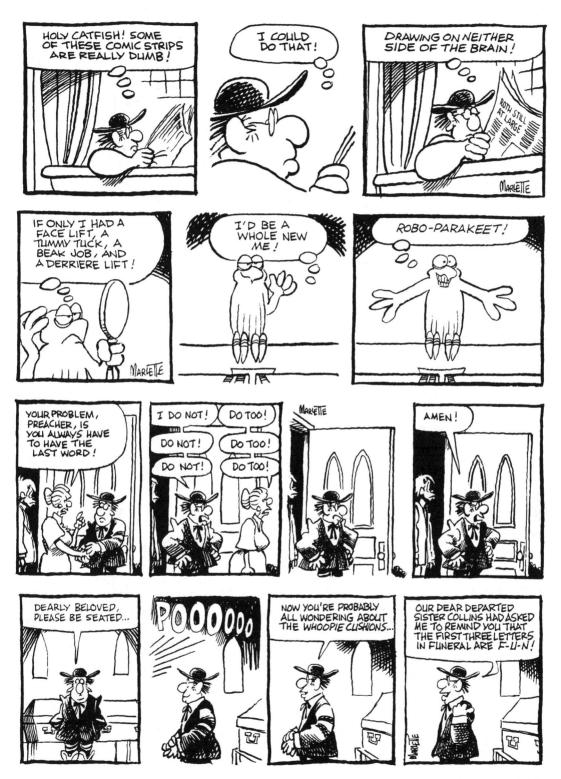

115

116

117

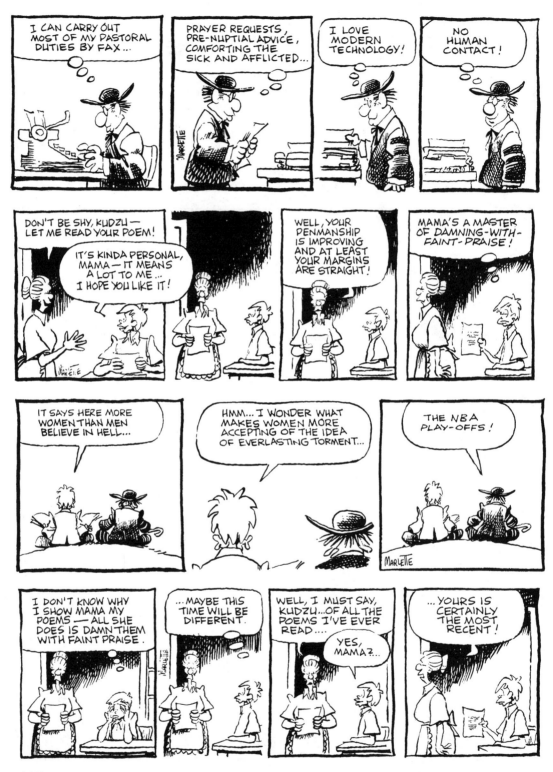

119

120

123

125

127

128

129

131

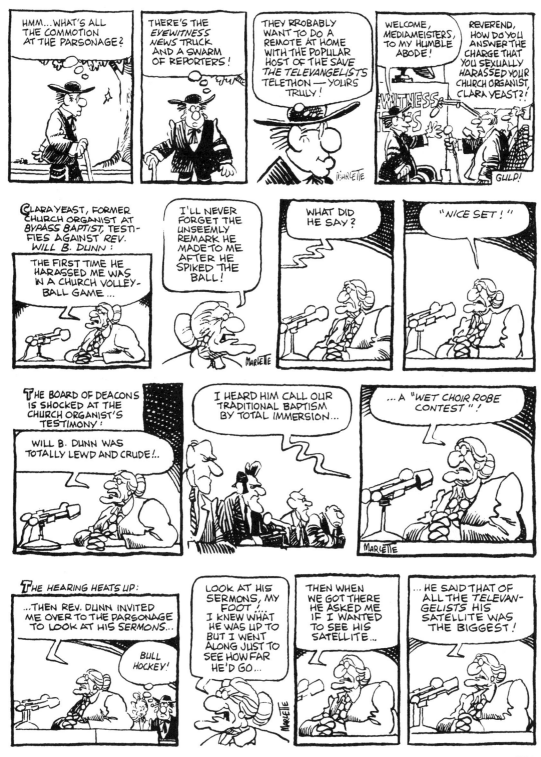

138

140

141

143

145

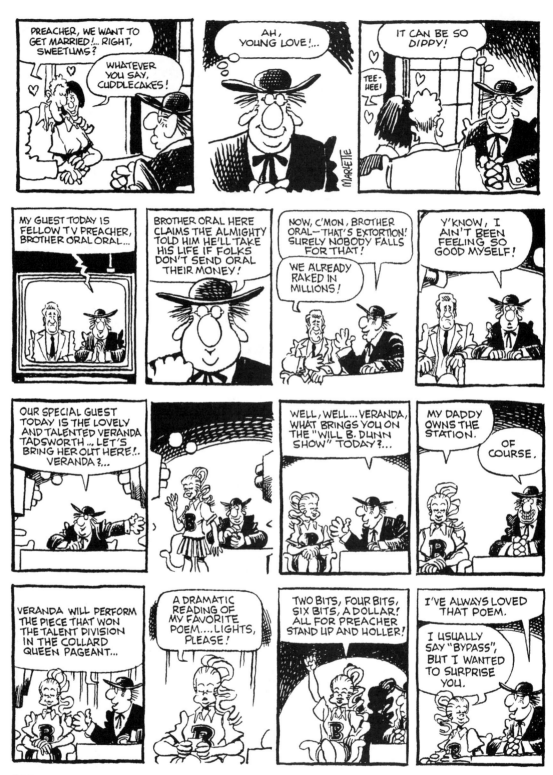

147

149

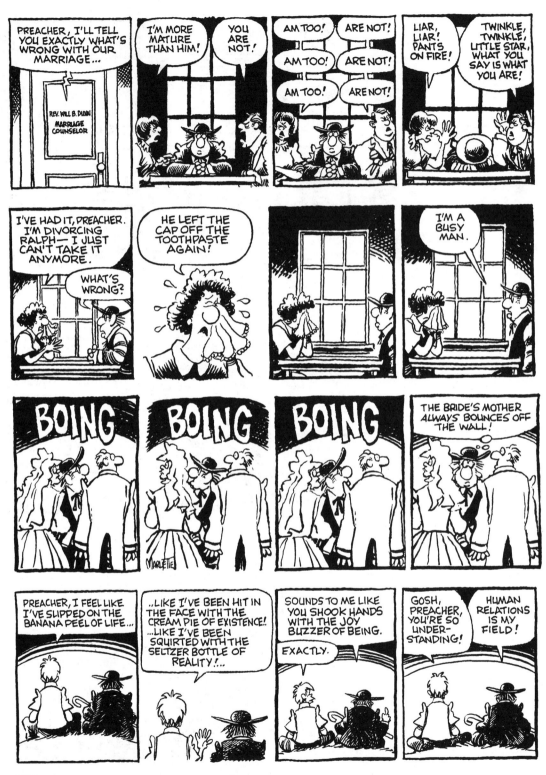

150

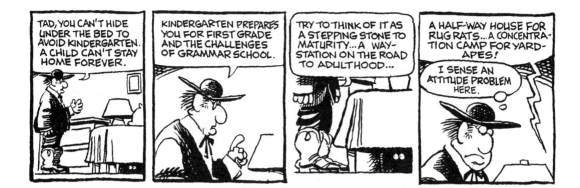

158

161

167

168

169

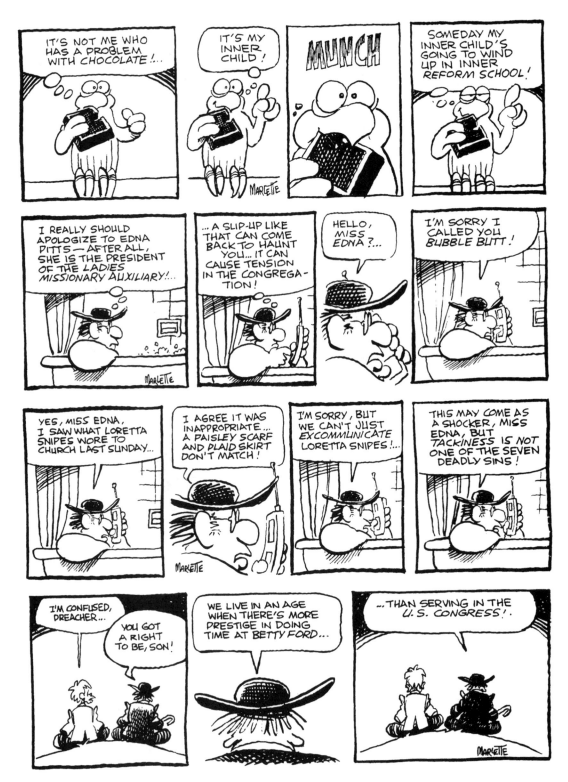

170

173

179

180